EMILY HEARN / MARK THURMAN

HELPING KIDS

DRAW

&Write

PICTURE BOOKS

EMILY HEARN / MARK THURMAN

HELPING KIDS

DRAW

&Write

PICTURE BOOKS

Pembroke Publishers Limited

- Draw & Write Your Own Picture Book
- Helping Kids Draw & Write Picture Books
- Illustration Ideas for Creating Picture Books

- Copyright 1990 Emily Hearn and Mark Thurman

Pembroke Publishers Limited
538 Hood Road
Markham, Ontario
L3R 3K9

Canadian Cataloguing in Publication Data

Hearn, Emily, 1925-
  Helping kids draw and write picture books

(Storyboarding)
Includes bibliographical references.
ISBN 0-921217-47-1

1. Picture-books - Technique - Study and teaching (Elementary). 2. Creative writing - Study and teaching (Elementary). 3. Picture-books for children - Authorship. I. Thurman, Mark, 1948-
II. Title. III. Series: Hearn, Emily, 1925-
Storyboarding.

PN147.5.H43 1990   808.06'8   C90-094790-X

Editor: Art Hughes
Designer: John Zehethofer
Typesetting: Jay Tee Graphics Ltd.

Printed and bound in Canada
0 9 8 7 6 5 4 3 2

CONTENTS

FOREWORD

The eight stages of storyboarding described in this book will help children design original picture books with exciting illustrations and creative stories.

The focus on the animator's map, or storyboard, is deliberate and unique. Its 24-frame pattern forces the young author/illustrator to jump right into the story, select only the most essential aspects of the plot, and when it's drawn, describe the actions and feelings of the characters in vivid, apt words.

The final storyboarding stages provide key directions for title selection, cover design, lettering styles, binding choices, and a *grand finale* of the gala publishing party and book sharing opportunities.

ACKNOWLEDGMENTS

We acknowledge gratefully Pam Erickson, whose insight inspired the project, Art Hughes and Les Parsons who made it happen in Scarborough schools, the Ontario Arts Council who funded us outside the Toronto area, Barbara Brunsden and Kathy Matsushita and all the energetic librarians and teachers who worked alongside us. And, most of all, the lively children whose fresh ideas continue to instruct us.

Storyboarding isn't the way books are written. Our adaptation of the animator's 'map' is an educational tool, pure and simple. It works at its richest with children nurtured on storytelling and process writing. Already in love with words, they enjoy discrimination in their use.

Based on our experience in numerous elementary and secondary school classrooms, this book offers critical information that will direct children to thoughtful writing and exciting illustrations. It will also encourage them to consider design as an essential feature of original picture books.

Do not be misled by what seems to be visual emphasis. Storyboarding means conceiving a plot in its entirety before a word is written. Drawn to show action that peaks and resolves, it eliminates the garrulous 'and then' and frees the writer to focus on language of sensibility and experience. It calls on skills allied to playwriting and poetry where words, few but apt, must resonate.

Focusing on 'camera angles' is not just for pleasing variety, but for knowledge of how pictures affect the viewer emotionally. A hidden aim is for children to acquire TV literacy by practising it and becoming aware of its influence on themselves.

ORIGIN OF THE STORYBOARDING APPROACH

Our storyboarding approach developed from an invitation to a high school where we were known to the students as the illustrator-writer team of the popular "Mighty Mites" feature in *Owl* magazine, as well as our own books. We advised students who were making picture books for a kindergarten they were 'twinning'. Their success with the process triggered storyboarding workshops for teachers, who were quick to pick up on its potential for pupils in much earlier stages of language learning.

After seven years of observing teachers carrying out our initial experiments, we know that the process works. Hence this book for you.

We want children to share our fun with story and design and color. We know they enjoy drawing and writing their own picture books, because we have cabinets bulging with photocopies, none of them substitutes for the colored, textured, subtle, poetic books that the young authors invariably want to keep. We don't ask for and haven't been offered a single one. Unspoken thanks.

Plenty of work lies ahead for you and your children and we wish you the same marvelous enjoyment that storyboarding projects have given us.

Eight Stages of Storyboarding Project

A storyboard is what you see on the last pages of this book. It is a series of white "frames" divided by black lines, each numbered frame representing a page of the planned book. In other words, a writer's storyboard is a kind of map or miniature plan of a book.

Eight stages carry the author/illustrator from stimulus to moment when photo and biography are pasted on the inside or outside of the back cover of the completed book. Done!

Some stages are deliberately rapid: others, as time-consuming as the writer/illustrator wishes.

The eight stages are detailed under the following headings:

ONE: Reading Picture Books as Stimulus
TWO: Ten Minutes for Story Collaboration
THREE: Storyboarding the Plot (Fast Pencil)
FOUR: Book Mock-up (Fast Pencil)
FIVE: Full-Color Book: Color, Detail, Cut-and-Paste, Collage
SIX: Writing the Story: Editing, Paste-up of Copy

SEVEN: Finishing Touches: Title, Cover Design, Dedication, Autobiography, Endpapers
EIGHT: Laminating, Binding, Protective Cover, Sharing

The project described in the *Storyboarding* series is based on a
24-page format (a total of 28 frames, including front and back covers
— inside and outside). For younger children the format may be modified to 12 pages (16 frames, including covers) or even 10 pages (14
frames).

Materials You'll Need

For Storyboarding

- storyboards on white paper

  *Photocopy only one storyboard
  for each team*, because children
  will be collaborating at this stage
  of the project.

- pencils

  For drawing 'how my characters
  really look'.

- erasers

- paper

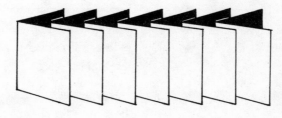

For Book Mock-up

- seven sheets of newsprint,
  roughly 45cm × 20 cm
  (18" × 8")

  Folded inside each other, not
  stapled or fastened together, *one
  book per team*.

- pencils

- erasers

For Full-Color Book

- seven sheets of colored manila or plain cartridge paper, same size as book mock-up

  One book for each person.

- colored markers

  Crayola water-based markers are best, because they don't bleed through the paper and they offer a wide range of brilliant primary and pastel shades.

- pencil crayons

  For fine, small detail.

- paint and brushes

- big and little cans of water

- lots of newspapers to protect desk/table surfaces and floors

  Many children enjoy the slosh of paint and put up happily with drying delays. If paper wets through, the simple expedient of pasting a fresh sheet on the back makes for a fat book but a fulfilled artist.

- oil pastels

  Oil pastels come in a wide variety of shades. Put clean paper between pages while the color 'sets', to avoid smudging. The colors will melt if the pages are laminated.

- chalk pastels

  Put paper between pages to prevent smudging, and remove it later.

For Texture and Collage

- scissors
- glue, paste, sticky tape, glue sticks
- construction paper (variety of colors)
- wallpaper samples
- gift wrappings
- magazines to cut up for pictures
- cotton batting
- cloth scraps, felt, velvet, satin, silk, patterned cotton
- egg cartons
- macaroni, fancy noodles
- wool, embroidery cotton, string, cord

Many wastebaskets, strategically placed!

For Cover and Binding

- cardboard
- bristol board
- heavy construction paper
- vinyl wallpaper
- thin plywood or wallboard
- stapler with long handle
- glue or glue sticks
- tape (preferably book-binding) in different colors
- wool, string, cord, or even dental floss

A cerlox or spiral binder and a laminating machine would be useful but are not really necessary.

Reading Picture Books as Stimulus

The title of Stage One says it all. Read and read and read and read to your children. Choose your own favorites because your enjoyment will be contagious and the publishing market continues to offer new delights.

Remember, when *we* conduct student workshops, we are extraterrestrials, not part of the family as you are, and our short visits need to make instant contact as well as impact. The tried-and-true books described here are not listed for you to use — some are out of print anyway — but the reasons for our choices may help you adapt your selection to feature the significant concepts. (Please consult the annotated list of recommended picture books at the end of this book.)

The first is *The Great Big Fire Engine Book* by Tibor Gergely. It exemplifies our main point that action drawing tells a story. Its large pages should be turned slowly, to the end, without reference to the few words printed at the bottom of the pages.

With a second showing of the book and a reading of the words, children will realize that by simple mimicry of sounds, "Crank, crank, up go the ladders", "Sput, sput, out goes the fire", the author-illustrator has evoked a dimension of 'you are there' experience impossible to pictures alone. Because very young children, like babies, are still grasping their environment through imitation of its sounds, the author has caught them where they are. The book, published in 1950, was an immediate hit with preschoolers and has been reprinted often.

This presentation is followed by a reading in tandem of two books for contrast, Joan Hanson's *I'm Going to Run Away* and Margaret

Wise Brown's *The Runaway Bunny*, the edition illustrated in 1972 by Clement Hurd. The mild shock of the running away from home theme makes direct impact. Each writer's reassuring handling of it makes contact. Vicariously, the presenter is 'in' with the children and secure enough with the group to make a few quick analyses. Two of these derive from Joan Hanson's book, where a line of witty text serves each large, colorfully illustrated page describing a very young runaway's selection of what he'll take with him.

First, it is a usual part of her plotting to draw a picture to a page but sometimes to make a 'double spread' of one picture across two facing pages, especially when the boy's need for a bigger bag culminates with the inclusion of a favorite apple tree. And, we add, "Soon you'll be planning pages like these."

The other point, crucial to plot structure, is that every story 'turns around'. Here the pivot is obvious to the youngest listener when the boy exclaims, "HEY, WAIT A MINUTE! I'm not running away from home. I'M TAKING IT WITH ME. I think I'll stay here. It's easier."

They recognize the turnaround when it comes in *The Runaway Bunny*, old hands at criticism now, and receptive to new observations, such as, there's no subject under the sun that hasn't been written. The difference is in how it's done. No other two books could show this better.

We capitalize on this observation by telling the group that some of them may hear others plot a similar theme to theirs, and accuse them of 'copying'. Oh sin! We guarantee that the way each collaborating pair writes and illustrates the story is going to make it as different as night and day from anyone else's. This is a failsafe guarantee because in a world of human variants it would be bizarre to find any two individuals craving to 'copy' the work of any two others. This is precisely why we recommend partners.

Teamwork is frequently part of original writing, especially in media. Two minds listening and making joint judgments enrich the end product. Children benefit from learning cooperation early in a fun activity that springs from the heart.

The Runaway Bunny is still the more common circumstance in picture book publishing, a book illustrated after it has been written by another person.

We call attention to the part where Clement Hurd has whimsically picked up on the mother rabbit who cautions, "If you become a fish in a trout stream, I will become a fisherman and I will fish for you." The illustrator depicts her luring the renegade with a carrot flung to him on a fishing line.

Children sense a challenge in the suggestion that sometimes two minds work better than one. At the end of the book, they observe where the illustrator's fancy has embellished that of the writer.

All good picture books reinforce these concepts. We end on a plane of fantasy or pure nonsense. The nub of truth is understood by all children as they cry or laugh with characters in the story.

You know many picture books like these that touch on realities beyond realism. Share them with children before turning them loose to writing.

Now, not to lose the emotional impetus of the picture book reading experience, we recommend that you launch into Stage Two of the storyboarding project as soon as possible.

Hints for the stimulus stage

- Read to children every day from a wide variety of stories and poems, especially your own favorites.

- Provide a library of picture books for student perusal and reading. Titles similar to those listed under Recommended Picture Books (pages 51-59) are exemplary because they illustrate the storytelling and design techniques described in this guide.

Ten Minutes for Story Collaboration

Partners have been chosen. Our preference is for friends to work together, because friends can argue differences of opinion without hurting one another's feelings. A 'truer' story is likely to spring from the affection of friends than from two children arbitrarily assigned to work with each other. The friendship grouping reinforces the tradition of a picture book being an affair of the heart.

We give the partners *only* ten minutes to walk around the room and talk about who their characters will be (anyone or anything at all but not from TV or other books), where the action will take place (anywhere), and what kind of difficulty will arise (no need for resolution yet).

No pencil and paper, just talk and feedback! And no adult interference. At this juncture it is vital that no one impedes the flow of spontaneous ideas. If, however, a team is having serious trouble and not getting anywhere, we ask them the basic questions: Who are your main characters? Where does the story take place? What is the problem?

A ten-minute deadline injects adrenalin, and having a partner as a baffleboard speeds the process of inspiration. Although the children are free to change their plot later, we are always astonished that practically every group sticks with the original plot that came hot off the griddle.

The group is gathered. One in each pair rapidly highlights characters, setting, difficulty, as we jot down the information in a notebook.

The purpose of oral reportage isn't for our sake. It's to provide an audience for friends whose ingenious ideas are already being reshaped and firmed up in the telling. Hearing others buoys up the less secure children.

To give you a sense of time-line, the readings, discussions, and plotting consultations take an hour to eighty minutes. You've lost the point of 'stimulus' if it drags out any longer than that.

Hints for the story collaboration stage

- Arrange for friends, not arbitrarily selected partners, to work together.

- Allow only a short period (ten minutes maximum) for partner decisions on characters, plot, setting, and the nature of the conflict (no need for resolution yet).

- Intervene only if a complete stalemate develops and ask a few key questions.

Storyboarding the Plot (Fast Pencil)

Big moment now! Hold up a storyboard and watch faces as you announce, "*This* is your book." Disbelief and dismay — is that all? — register on *every* face. "Not really, but it is a 'map', or miniature plan, of your book. Soon you'll be drawing stick figures or circle characters in these frames to show your whole story."

Reference to camera angles is an essential preliminary to successful storyboarding. (The main points of view are presented in miniature in the appendix section entitled Illustration Ideas.)

A display of large posters showing different points of view would be particularly effective at this stage in the storyboarding project. We recommend introducing the *horizontal* point of view first — with characters or objects placed along the 'horizon' — and explaining that this is the usual method a child would choose to illustrate an everyday scene. In fact, most children use the horizontal view exclusively. We also point out that important figures should be reasonably large and placed in the middle of the scene, not miniscule shapes along the bottom edge of the page or frame.

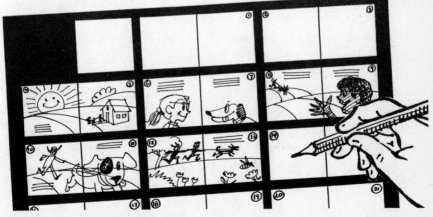

Various arrangements of *foreground, midground,* and *background* (coming towards the viewer as well as going away) should be illustrated and discussed before any introduction of the dramatic *close-up* or *extreme close-up* or the more innovative *bird's-eye* and *ant's-eye* viewpoints.

Each camera angle affects the viewer differently: the coolly horizontal, the angled bird's-eye overview, or the ant's-eye underview with its crushing sense of power, the close-up — most emotional of all. Watch TV with the sound off. Where is the camera in each shot?

Plant the suggestion that they'll be varying their own 'shots' for the particular effect they want when they do their own storyboards. If you think this is too sophisticated for them, remember that all these children are constantly watching TV, where shooting is choreographed for maximum stimulus. After they have viewed TV for a while with the sound off, their drawings prove how high their visual awareness already is. As young as seven and eight, they are happily varying angles and filling page space with a sense of design.

Display the posters on points of view prominently in the workroom — on a bulletin board, on a chalkrail, or on the ledge above the chalkboard — until the end of the project. Posters illustrating collage and lettering styles may be added to the display later.

Also mention the suspense of a page turn. This is particularly apparent in a 'pattern book' where the answer to a repeated question isn't given until the page is turned and a hundred possibilities for it have been prompted.

Time-line consideration again! We've reached what has to be a break time for the children — a recess or an overnight. Then allot no more than 45-60 minutes for storyboarding. Why? Because this is mind-clearing, a pinning down of essentials. If you allow endless time, you're going to have every hair on a character's head exquisitely curled — and no plot.

The storyboard, which you can copy from the one provided at the end of this guide, is a grid of 28 squares, or 'frames', the first representing the front cover, the last, the back cover. Intervening frames are paired for double-page spreads, with a wide black line between each pair, signifying the all-important page turn. The frames numbered from #4 - #24 are the actual frames in which the children draw their story. The rest, as shown, will be endpapers, copyright and dedication page, and title page.

Because, at the outset, two children are collaborating on the project, they are given *only one* storyboard between them. Before they begin, remind them of the importance of camera angles, filling the space, page-turn suspense, and having no words recorded. Then, with sharpened pencils and fresh erasers, they are ready to start.

Sometimes both children draw, often only one, but either way they plot together. We suggest they put a small X on frames #12/13 to indicate that their story needs to be at its most difficult here (or somewhere in this line of frames). The worst has happened. How will the characters survive or solve their problems?

They can begin drawing story action in frames #4 and #5 or start at dilemma point (frames #12/13) and go through to the end before tackling the opening. Some catch on readily to this upheaval of usual progression, some are alarmed, but all are made aware, simply by its mention, that openings must not be labored.

This hurdles the familiar pitfall of most neophyte writers, a state analogous to falling in love, so delightful you don't want it to end, but alas, boring to the reader who needs to have your marvelous character shown in excited action, not painstakingly 'introduced'. No more awakenings to the alarm, admirable teeth-brushing, and saying goodbye to Mom. Stories need trouble and complication, please, soon!

Offer sparing guidance, if any, during the initial storyboarding. You'll help with the editing when the storyboard is finished.

Two basic rules! *Don't draw on children's work* (demonstrate on a separate piece of paper or on a blank storyboard) and *don't tamper with their story ideas*, unless you sense total confusion or lazybrain. The adult role is to preserve the originality of thought by helping children express it to maximum effect.

While some children are waiting and drawing on scrap paper 'how their characters will really look' or finishing their storyboarding, we take a team aside for a private session and sit between the partners who alternate in telling their story as we point to each drawing frame by frame.

We watch for clarity, drama, flow and variety. Does the plot turn around? We have on hand another blank storyboard on which they can redraw frames that could be interchanged, or eliminated if redundant. This avoids the dismal feeling that alteration means doing the whole thing over. They append this to the original. Some will cut out the revised frames and glue them over the old ones.

Any redrawing is usually for more use of the intimate close-up and for a shift from constant horizontal, midground renderings to angled views, such as bird's-eye or ant's-eye. Scrunchy little figures along the bottom of the frame are shoved up to the middle where they gain significance and fill the space. Double-page spreads are suggested where they may lend emphasis.

This review exposes the occasional circumstance when a partner has slackened off or when one has dominated to such an extent that the other scarcely knows what's going on. It's good to catch this early since the partners will be completing their final books individually. Conferencing may work without anything more needing to be said.

Drawing characters as they'll really look, referred to earlier, is practice for the next stage, the book mock-up, where the characters won't be circle or stick figures any more. Using partners as models, children draw them upside down, from the back, above, below, talking to friends, angry, sad, kicking a football — anything but simply smiling straight at the viewer.

To avert the disappointment of a lost story, we recommend at this stage the photocopying of a master set of the completed storyboards.

Hints for the storyboarding stage

- Begin with a poster demonstration of camera angles. After discussing the various viewpoints, display the posters prominently in the children's work area.

- Emphasize the importance of using a variety of camera angles, or viewpoints, and the reasons for each.

- Since the focus is on action, not talking heads, remind the children that the bodies must show what's happening by the way they move and relate to each other.

20

- Stick or circle figures with no detail are most suitable for the fast-pencil work of storyboarding.

- Since readers will be interested primarily in the characters and what happens to them, children should make them large, filling up the entire page. Too often, young illustrators have a tendency to draw small figures along the bottom of the frame (and later the page).

- Advise children to jump into their story feet first and capture interest by providing trouble and complication as soon as possible.

- The double-page spread, with drawings and text spread across facing pages, can be very effective, but the large space requires careful planning. Even when the individual page has a separate image, its design also must be planned in relation to that of its facing page. This will produce continuity in viewing as well as in reading.

- The suspense of a page turn is an important consideration, especially in a 'pattern' book.

- Although it should not require repeating at this stage, remind the author/illustrator that *no words* go on the storyboard, just lines to indicate where the words will go later.

Book Mock-Up (Fast Pencil)

An edited storyboard catapults a pair of author/illustrators into the fourth stage, receipt of a newsprint book, called the 'mock-up'. It is the same size that the finished one will be, seven pages, 45 cm × 20 cm (18" × 8"). Folded, this becomes a 24-page book (plus covers, endpapers, publisher's information page, and title page) that is 23 cm × 20 cm (9" × 8").

Pages should be numbered so that 12/13 is the centrefold. Drawings will begin on the double spread of pages 4 and 5.

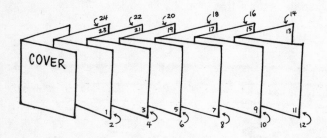

Don't staple these books. Since two children are working on one book, they will take separate pages to draw simultaneously, using their common storyboard for reference, matching page and frame numbers. (Later, they will have their own books.)

This is fast-pencil work, loose and rapid, without words, images filling the space, adapting the pictures on storyboard frames to full-book pages. The emphasis is on design, seeing the unity of a double-page spread, or when there are single-page drawings, keeping an eye on how they balance the work on the facing page.

Be on the lookout for children who forget to transfer a double-page spread on the storyboard to *two* pages in the book mock-up, thereby throwing out the page order as well as losing the impact of the spread.

Discourage time-consuming detail. Only major shapes and important objects would be outlined. Just like the storyboard, the book mock-up will be edited later and changes made, if desired.

STURDY FOLDER FOR BITS AND PIECES

Often two children take their pages home to complete before the next session. A wise precaution is to supply each team with a sturdy folder, large enough to keep all the bits and pieces involved in the project. This cuts down on loss and also becomes a telling record of effort and planning when, finally, the day comes that laminated, titled books are in their hands — detailed, colored, vividly written, with their own names on the cover as authors and illustrators. All the rough work and first drafts will help them to see how far they've come.

EDITING THE BOOK MOCK-UP

Editing the book mock-up is conducted in the same way as editing the storyboard, in private sessions. Since the storyline was firmly established when the storyboard was edited, the book mock-up stage is purely visual.

- Do the drawings fill up the space or is there a yawning gap?

- Do some of the characters need to be made bigger?

- Are they well up from the bottom of the page?

- Do their bodies show action?

- Do the characters relate to each other?

One sheet of newsprint paper (60 cm × 45 cm or 24" × 18") may be cut into three pieces (20 cm × 45 cm or 8" × 18"), as shown. When folded in half, each of these will become four pages. You will therefore need seven newsprint pieces (20 cm × 45 cm or 8" × 18") for a book mock-up, six pieces to make the inside (24 pages) and one piece to make the cover.

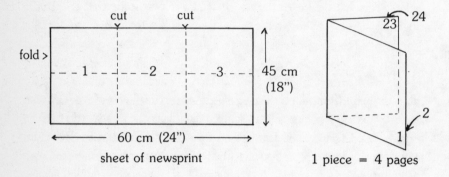

sheet of newsprint   1 piece = 4 pages

Hints for the book mock-up stage

* Make sure the pages get numbered correctly, with pages 12 and 13 as the centrefold.

* Don't staple these newsprint books, especially if two children are working as partners and using a common storyboard as reference. They will have individual books at the next stage.

* The emphasis is on design, without words and without detail, images filling the space.

* Check to make sure children transfer a double-page spread on the storyboard to *two* pages in the book mock-up.

* Supply a sturdy folder for each set of partners to help them keep track of the numerous bits and pieces of artwork.

* Assist with the editing of the mock-up in private sessions with each team, asking the children to answer the key questions: Do the drawings fill up the space? Do the bodies show action? Do the characters relate to each other?

Full-Color Book

Quantities of exuberant color and collage material are on hand. Your room should look as if a color cyclone had hit. The person who just provides non-messy pencil crayons is short-changing the children woefully, as two identical, uninspired copies of the book mock-up will reveal.

Each child receives a book of good quality manila or cartridge paper, same size, same number of pages as the mock-up, which, to avoid mix-ups, is promptly numbered in the same way — in pencil for now. Later, proud authors will ink and style them in keeping with their illustrations. (Manila paper comes in a variety of colors, but cartridge paper is white.)

Abundant color choice brings out each partner's individuality. Show the items available and make it clear that everything can be mixed and matched to anyone's desire. And watch what happens.

Cut-and-paste enthusiasts will make a dash for the fancy papers, wools, and spaghetti. Others will rush for paint and pastels, many for markers. The sound level rises, happily.

The born illustrator, ignoring all of this, will set to with single-minded vigor, likely with marker or crayon, content to recreate an already fine mock-up. However, in the buzz and stir that collage activity is creating, this person will deign to look around to see what is happening. When a child like this acknowledges the potential of mixing draftsmanship with collage, the results can be phenomenally imaginative.

For many children, collage provides a rich outlet for artistic expression. Remember that the mock-up they follow has already been edited for balanced design. Whole shapes cut from paper now represent characters; exotic backgrounds are derived from fancy papers or magazine photos; even pop-ups, see-throughs, pull-downs, or fold-outs may be added. Their books can be spectacularly inventive.

Also, the tactile manipulation of cotton, artificial fur, wools, etc. for small detail continues to deepen the attachment to 'my book'. This, in our own absolutely unfounded theory, develops sensitivity in their choice of language later. For this reason we leave story-writing to the very end.

Storyboarding is for all children, whatever their artistic or writing skills. Its aim is expression, not achievement compared to someone else's. Because its subject matter is past childhood, even a seven-year-old is motivated to create pleasure out of it for a younger person.

Expect a mess, but watch the enthusiasm, concentration, and sheer pleasure children experience as they set to their tasks with meticulous vigor. When the ban on detail is lifted, self-directed perfectionism takes over.

It may take over half an hour to paste each strand of yellow string for the mermaid's hair and sheathe her fishtail in macaroni scales, but let it happen and face the inevitable. *Large quantities of time* need to be allowed from now to the completion of the project. Children can take their books home overnight or on weekends. Pride usually protects against carelessness.

You will observe variations in most partners' work. Although both are following the same storyboarding design and basic theme of the mock-up and a few still conform to each other's ideas, most see the use of color as a chance to diverge. They already know that they will be writing their own story and that their title and cover will be their own inventions.

One child may stay with line work; another blend it with collage; one may choose pastel; another, pop-ups or fold-outs. Feelings about color and texture are so personal that wide variety results. Sly jabs of wit surface unexpectedly — in slogans on T-shirts, in posters on bedroom walls, or blazoned on street signs.

You are the monitor who provides supplies, gives attentive help when asked, but doesn't instruct. Not here! What you've wanted all along for children is happening, an outpouring of exuberant originality. Let it be!

Hints for the full-color book stage

- Have on hand an abundant supply of coloring and collage materials, the greater the variety the better.

- Supply each child with a book of good quality manila or cartridge paper, the same size and with the same number of pages as the book mock-up.

- To avoid later mix-ups, have the children number the pages immediately, matching the numbers exactly with those in the book mock-up.

Writing the Story

A complete, colored picture book is in the child's hands. It tells a story, but lacks intensity of feeling. It needs words. We sense excitement in a character's situation, but excitement alone wears thin. We want to identify 'on the inside'.

We ask the children to put the book away for a few days, then to leaf through it is as if someone else had created it. If tape recorders are available, let them make an 'off-the-top' spoken version. Put the tape away, for later reference, if wanted. This is quite literally an exercise 'for the record', not a text of the final words of their story. But this reading, with or without being recorded, has fixed essentials in their minds.

Now at last they write. We usually supply another blank storyboard. Older children print small enough that significant language fits into the frames that correspond to their pictures. This often works with younger ones, too, who don't naturally resort to a lot of words anyway.

The medium is indeed the message. What we are trying to avoid is handing them the familiar piece of lined paper and saying, "Now go to it!" Lined paper tends to make them revert to 'once upon a time. . . and then. . . and then', forgetting to keep a taut relationship with what they've just drawn.

But if they start with the storyboard, and then take more paper, on their own they put down the page numbers. Now they're keeping a focus, reflected in acute language.

We ask them to feel that they themselves are experiencing the drama of each page. What do they hear? see? taste? smell? How would they feel? Sad? confused? happy? angry? scared? We need to know. Because they have been 'playing' so long with their characters, dressing and animating them, devising stage sets, children heed this call for sensory words. It is their daily life after all, and they like giving its vitality back to the reader.

We ask the children to write in full sentences. Otherwise, they might be tempted to think of their books as comic strips, with balloons for 'Oh no! What next!' This would be fine, if these balloons were in addition to a fully told story, but they are not adequate on their own.

This might be the place to say that when schools include 'special ed' children in our groups we couldn't tell you first or last which ones they are. There is a wholeness to creative ventures that can't be measured on scales.

We live in a community where children of many nationalities arrived as recently as yesterday. Planes bring newcomers weekly from El Salvador, Somaliland, Iraq, Hong Kong, Vietnam, India, the West Indies, Greece, and other parts of Europe. As soon as they arrive they are in school. Few speak English. All can draw. We ask a receptive couple to take in one of them so that immersion in our culture can be self-expression. They are encouraged to write the drawn story in their own language, if they wish.

Most schools have access to typewriters or word processors. Children in older grades or parents may volunteer to help. When you have coaxed out language that has flow and vitality, and have arranged for editing of spelling and grammar — the story can be printed, cut, and pasted in the appropriate spaces. Children consider this very professional and like the clean look of the finished page.

If you know beforehand that typed copy will not be possible, remember the suggestions we made at the earlier design stage for drawing lines to represent where the words will go later. The edited words can be printed neatly in these spaces.

Student Titles and Plots

These titles are the selection of just one Grade 2-3 class, not as you may think, our Choice Hits culled over the years. All groups do this when encouraged and caught up in class contagion — poetry, of a kind.

THE BOY AND THE CRICKET PERSON
FRIDAY SPOOKS
GREEN DINOSAUR
MOUSE MEASLES
UNDER THE UNDERWATER
THE EGG WAR
THE LITTLE WITCH THAT WANTED
TO BE A NORMAL GIRL
WHO DO MY PARENTS THINK
THEY ARE?
COME BACK, FLUFFY
THE FAIRIES OF THE LAND

From our million notes of children's plots, we are passing on some that demonstrate the high-powered imagination you can expect. They come as hot-off-the-top response to stimulus and, with only ten minutes allowed, weren't watered down by sobering thoughts. The children who do change their plots recognize that the original wasn't strong enough in the first place. The reverse doesn't happen when they catch on to a blithe attitude accepting that *anything goes*.

SOME ARE EXOTIC

— on a purple moon, a gigantic sneaker loses its foot
— an alien Santa Claus and a 'real' one stage a fight
— Cleopatra, the Sphinx, and a Pyramid have their heads exchanged in a whirlwind
— a baby longs for a house made of apples
— a penguin suffers sunburn on its back

- a frog, a toad, and a dragonfly destroy a city
- three fairies are trapped in a rosebud
- a runaway city drives to New York
- two hungry mice are tossed into space by the moon, when it discovers they think it's made of green cheese

MANY ARE IN OUTER SPACE

- a child asks his mom if he can go to Mars, she says 'no', he goes anyway
- robots and boys navigate rival spaceships to Neptune
- three kids, on what's left of Earth, defend it against a robot enemy
- three astronauts save a city in the Universe from aliens armed with deadly weapons
- friendly Martians guide lost Earth-children home

MANY INVOLVE TECHNOLOGY

Stories abound of mad scientists, wayward computers, wizards who betray children into hapless crises in complicated time warps.

Others, with less sophistication, merrily combine heroic warriors with dinosaurs and kangaroos with pterodactyls.

ANIMALS

Legendary, real, or stuffed animals are all-time favorite heroes, especially with the youngest writers. Exploits thinly disguise their day-to-day concerns and ambitions in the social world of home and school.

- Henry Horse wears a dunce cap because his writing is sloppy
- a giraffe is called bad names because of its long neck
- a unicorn and a cat become movie stars
- a rooster talks too much
- a teddy bear is frightened of the dark and something in the closet
- a kangaroo can't hop and a girl helps it learn
- a dolphin and speckled trout save a fisherman's life
- a mouse doesn't want to go to school
- a lion cub runs away from a circus

Hints for the writing stage

- Children have already done the basic planning on their storyboards — characters and setting selected, conflict established, plot developed, solution provided. Remind them, then, that what the text provides is depth or intensity of feeling.

- Emphasize the need for sensory detail. What do the characters see, hear, taste, smell? How do they feel?

- Require statements in full sentences. The children are not just adding words in comic strip balloons.

- Encourage children in older grades or parents to assist with typing or word processing as well as with the editing of spelling, grammar, and basic punctuation.

Finishing Touches

All children have had a title in their minds, even before they knew how their story would end, but we have discouraged them from putting it on the book mock-up or final cover. Until now. Because with the book 'inside' they can conjure up a better one. We ask them to scan library shelves and note which titles make them want to look inside the book. Whatever the content, the title has done its job, teased them in.

We suggest they dream up five likely titles, then choose the pithy one. This shatters them so much it does pull away the factual one they've been cherishing like an old coat. It probably reads 'Trouble with. . .' or 'Mystery of. . .' or 'Supercarrot to the Rescue. . . .' It may be one that features the name of the main character, or, horrors, something like 'Alfred Learns His Lesson'.

These are titles with the deflated power of clichés. Often they moralize, reveal the plot before the reader embarks on it, or name people who aren't interesting. The reader has to gamble that they will be, which is fine if the book is part of an established series.

Questions can be good: 'Was That a UFO?', 'What Happened to My Tail?' or ones featuring unlikely concepts: 'The Peanut Butter Surprise', 'Night Juggler', 'Green Santa Claus', or ones hinting at the ominous: 'Dark Castles', 'Boogie Under the Bed', or magic: 'The Magic Smelly Pair of Sneakers', or straight adventure: 'Animals' Escape', 'Little Lost Tiger', 'The Mosquito Coast', 'Wanted: A Round Black Spot (Reward).' These are examples from only two groups of children.

"What's going on?" you ask, and look inside to discover. Once an effective title is found, the cover can be designed. Sometimes the cover design is a repetition of a picture inside, but more often it's seen as a last challenge because, after all, it is the *grand finale* of the whole effort. The adventurous may design it to 'wrap around' and include the back cover.

The actual title must be printed *large* and *clear*, whether it is in a fancy style or plain. So must the names of the author and illustrator.

The inside of the front cover and its facing page as well as the inside of the back cover are reserved as 'endpapers' for those who still want to adorn their books. This is definitely optional. These can be abstract or geometric patterns drawn or done in collage. They may incorporate an image symbolizing the theme or setting of the story, for example, sailboats in a seagoing tale, weird aliens in a space one.

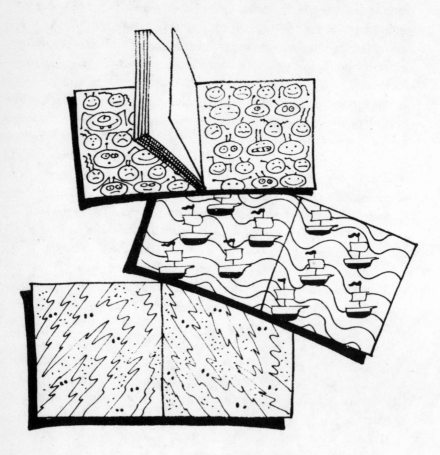

Page 2 is the publisher's information page. At the top goes the copyright, a small 'c' enclosed in a circle © followed by the author's name AS WELL AS THE PARTNER'S. Since the basic idea was both of theirs, it should be acknowledged here. The copyright symbol, followed by the year in which the work was completed, establishes ownership.

Below this, but larger on the page, the author may write THIS BOOK IS DEDICATED TO: or simply DEDICATED TO: followed by the name of a best friend, parent, relative, favorite teacher, even pet.

On the next page, page 3, the title, without illustration, is printed in clear, plain print, along with the author's name and that of the illustrator if someone else did the artwork. The names of both partners are not needed here or on the cover, unless the children themselves want it that way.

A brief autobiography, INFORMATION ABOUT THE AUTHOR AND THE ILLUSTRATOR, featuring favorite activities, friends, etc., is prepared. This, along with a photo of the author, is pasted on the back cover, on the inside, if the cover is a wraparound design, or even on the endpaper (page 1) at the beginning of the book.

Hints for the finishing touches stage

- Encourage children to invent an original title (just as they did for their plot), not something adapted from TV or other books.

- Suggest that the cover design be planned as a *grand finale* to sum up the whole story.

- Show them different lettering styles and have them print the title and the author's name large and clear in a suitable style.

- Remind them that the endpapers provide another opportunity for creative expression.

Binding and Sharing

If you have access to a laminating machine, by all means use it, at least for the covers of these precious books. Collage work is difficult to laminate, but such work is a product of much glue and material, both of which are preservatives on their own.

You're in for a big stapling or stitching job. Since most children can't handle this at all, teachers turn to volunteers for help. The best material, we are told, is dental floss, or fine string. A stapler needs to have a long handle.

If you feel that you want a protective outside cover, these are the steps to follow:

1. Cut an endpaper sheet the same height as the content pages but slightly wider.

2. With string, dental floss, or wool, sew the content pages to the endpaper sheet, as shown.

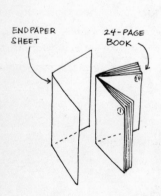

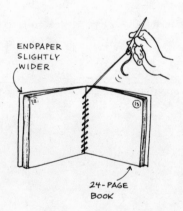

3. Cut a cover sheet the same height as the endpaper sheet but slightly wider and fold it in half.

4. Glue outside of endpaper sheet (with content pages attached) to inside of cover.

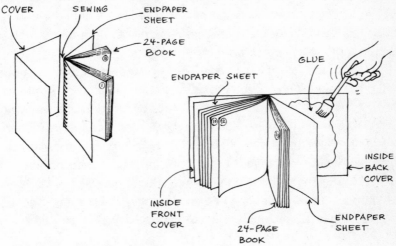

Voilà! The published book!

When the books are done, HAVE A PUBLISHING PARTY. We do, so should they. In a festive atmosphere of food and drink, streamers and balloons, invited parents and guests, a justly rewarding formality may be established for the proceedings.

This is the time for SHARING BOOKS. If many groups are participating, you can split up the partners, who take their books to join others in a circle of six or seven, show them the pictures, read the stories, and exchange anecdotes of the experience.

If it's a small group, both partners can stand, books facing the audience, and as one reads the text the other turns corresponding pages in his/her book. If their written versions are very different, have both read right through.

To crown the occasion, we find the right moment to ask a pair to hold up the storyboard that initiated their splendors. Even though we dimly remember that some time back it all did begin with a ten-minute idea pencilled on a grid of squares, a powerful surge of awareness affects everyone now.

These children have come through a process of conceptual planning, self-generated meticulousness, and writing for immediacy that has proven them to be what we are celebrating, AUTHORS AND ILLUSTRATORS.

Most children will want to keep their own books in the long run but are happy to have them circulate in the library until the end of the school year. They welcome every chance to read them to children in kindergarten and primary grades.

Later they may storyboard other books on their own, but it is more likely that they will have internalized its story-shaping concept and adapt it to future writing. This has always been our aim and hope.

You will find it useful to have storyboards on hand as reminders in other projects that this might be a first stage in planning their form. You may want to change it to an appropriate size and number of frames. For younger children the format may be modified to 12 pages (16 frames, including covers) or even 10 pages (14 frames). See the sample storyboards provided in the appendix.

Hints for the binding and sharing stage

- Seek assistance from older children with the laminating or binding of the final books.

- Plan a gala publishing party at which the authors/illustrators can show and read their books to parents, friends, classmates, and children of other grades.

Illustration Ideas

The design concepts presented in this illustration glossary are intended to help the inexperienced author/illustrator discover interesting, unusual, and dynamic ways to illustrate a picture book. They are grouped under three headings — points of view, collage, and design.

Suggestions under points of view progress from the *horizontal*, which children use almost exclusively for their pictures, to the more unusual *bird's-eye* and *ant's-eye* to the *extreme close-up* with its accentuated details and concentrated focus, potentially the most powerful of all.

The many different techniques for collage appeal to the author/illustrator who exclaims, "But I can't draw!" Some of these techniques are surprisingly simple, involving only cutting and rearranging colored paper or pictures. Some, however, are challenging, such as cutting out silhouettes and placing them on cutout landscape or juxtaposing positive and negative shapes.

Design considerations include deciding on type (word) placement, planning a cover, and selecting or inventing lettering. This section concludes with suggestions for cutting out letters and numbers — cutting colored paper into strips to ensure uniform letter height and cutting 'closed-in' letters (A, B, D, etc.) without folding the paper.

Points of view
HORIZONTAL

The horizontal view (along the horizon) is frequently used to make a normal, everyday picture and suits a fairly calm or passive moment in a story. For more emotional or dramatic moments, other points of view should be considered.

Points of view
FOREGROUND, MIDGROUND, BACK-GROUND
(Coming Towards You)

The most important character should be placed up close, in the foreground, and made larger than the others. Thus, when this character is approaching, the facial expression is more likely to catch the viewer's attention.

Points of view
FOREGROUND, MIDGROUND, BACKGROUND
(Going Away)

When characters face away from the viewer, the emotional intensity diminishes. This arrangement of foreground, midground, and background creates an impression that the action is passing by.

Points of view
BIRD'S-EYE

The bird's-eye view is an overview that shows where the action is taking place. From above, the viewer sees everything that's going on but is, for the moment, safely removed from any danger in the action below. What an unusual sense of power this creates!

Points of view
ANT'S-EYE

The ant's-eye view may be likened to that of small children who, of physical necessity, must look up at much of their surroundings. Adults must seem like giants. This viewpoint, then, tends to diminish the power of the viewer.

Points of view
CLOSE-UP
(Full Face — Part of a Sequence)

By focusing or concentrating the viewer's attention, the close-up often conveys intense emotion, especially if it is a double-page spread. It can be used frequently once the full features of the character have been established.

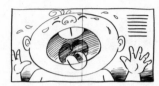

Points of view
CLOSE-UP
(Full Face — Front View)

The close-up, especially if it's a face, confronts the viewer. This is like having someone standing very close and then suddenly moving into your personal space. All your senses become alert at once!

Points of view
CLOSE-UP
(Four Designs)

Whether on a single page or part of a double-page spread, the close-up gets the viewer involved: "What's the matter with this baby? Why is it crying so hard?"

Points of view
EXTREME CLOSE-UP
(Side View — Cropped)

Extreme close-ups are frequently cropped. This means that the full picture would extend beyond the page or illustration border. These can be very dramatic, particularly if they are faces expressing intense emotion.

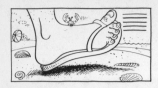

Points of view
EXTREME CLOSE-UP
(With Background Details)

An extreme close-up doesn't always have to be a face — it can be a finger pointing in a crucial direction, a hand turning a strange door knob, or a raised foot on a sandy beach. In such cases, background details contribute to the overall impression.

Points of view
FOREGROUND
(Six Views)

By rearranging three elements (person, house, and tree), the artist alters the composition to emphasize the important foreground subject. Since foreground objects are generally darker than background ones, they have been shaded.

Collage
CUTOUT
(With Face Details)

Simple shapes, which are easy to cut out, can turn into a moustache, eyebrows, eyes, or a bow tie when glued to a basic head outline. This technique gives maximum design effect with minimum effort.

Collage
CUTOUT
(With Patterned Paper)

Cutout pieces of patterned paper (wallpaper, gift wrapping, or even patterned cloth) can be arranged to create a colorful and dramatic scene. A dark-colored background will enhance the design by making the various elements stand out.

Collage
CUTOUT
(Interior Perspective)

Interior designs have foreground, mid-ground, and background areas just as outdoor settings have. The proximity, however, makes the handling of interior perspective more difficult.

Collage
CUTOUT
(Wavy Lines)

A simple yet effective underwater scene may be created by cutting a large sheet of blue construction paper into wavy strips, separating these slightly, and mounting them on a light-colored background. Words in air bubbles (where else?) and elements of Neptune's world may be added, as desired.

Collage
CUTOUT
(Silhouette on Drawn Landscape)

Black paper silhouette cutouts can be used to create dramatic foreground and background effects. Varying textures of grass, distant fields, buildings, and sky may be conveyed by a combination of lines, dots and shapes.

Collage
CUTOUT
(Positive and Negative Shapes)

Unusual effects may be achieved by planning a collage so that both the cutout parts (the positive shapes) and the remaining open spaces (the negative shapes) are utilized.

Collage
CUTOUT
(Parts Rearranged)

One way to make an original piece of art or a magazine picture more interesting or dynamic is to give it movement. The image may be cut into horizontal or vertical strips, which are separated slightly, moved to right or left, and mounted on a lighter or contrasting background.

Collage
CUTOUT AND TORN SHAPES

Drawing and printing with white pencil crayon on black paper can produce some unusual images. These, combined with cutout and torn shapes, may be mounted on a light or contrasting background for spectacular results.

Collage
CUTOUT
(Photo and Drawing Combined)

A collage of carefully selected magazine pictures, cartoon cutouts, word balloons, and comic strip lettering (newspaper headlines would do as well) is made to order for the person who exclaims, "But I can't draw!"

Design
TYPE PLACEMENT
(Seven Positions)

Words, also called type or text, are usually placed at the top of an illustrated page, but this is not a fixed rule. They can go anywhere as long as a space has been left for them, but they should never be squeezed in as an afterthought.

44

Design
COVER DESIGNS
(Four Examples)

Designing the cover usually comes last (along with the title) in a book-making project. Whether a repetition of a picture from inside the book or a totally new illustration, the cover design should be regarded as a *grand finale*.

Design
LETTERING STYLES

Since many words have their own visual characteristics, a lettering style may be selected or designed to give a word personality. The individual letters, however, must be legible and the words recognizable.

Cutout Lettering

Having children cut out letters is a useful exercise in small muscle control and helps with alphabet and word recognition.

In the storyboarding project, cutout letters can be used for the cover, title page, and special effects (sounds, for example) anywhere in the book.

Since most children have difficulty cutting out letters, we have selected block lettering, the simplest design for this activity.

These are the steps for children to follow:

1. Choose colored construction paper that suits the story (blue, if it takes place at sea or in the water; yellow, in the bright sun; green, in lush meadows or deep forest, etc.).

2. Cut strips of paper the appropriate height and width for the letters needed. A little extra allows for "mistakes" or miscalculations. The strip ensures that all letters will be uniform in height.

3. Cut the strips into blocks for letters of different widths. Remember that an 'M' is wider than an 'O' and that an 'I' is thinner than an 'F'.

4. Note the different ways of cutting the letter 'A', depending on whether a block or a triangular shape is desired.

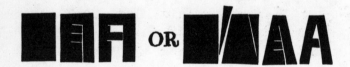

5. Cut 'closed-in' letters (A, B, D, O, P, Q, and R) without folding the paper. The outline letters below show where the scissors have *overcut* their mark, which is good because this ensures that the inside or enclosed pieces will fall out easily.

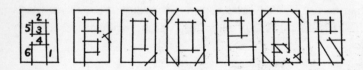

The overcuts, by the way, will not show up when the letter parts are pressed together and glued down, as seen below.

ABDOPQR

Block lettering

1. Block lettering is the easiest shape to cut out with scissors.

ABCDEF
GHIJKLM
NOPQRS
TUVWXYZ
& ?!.,
12345
67890

2. Here are some different ways to cut the letter 'S'. (These cutting techniques apply to all letters.)

3. Remember to vary the size and to use lowercase (small) letters for contrast.

Important Words

The following glossary defines important words that you will encounter when working with children to help them create their own picture books.

ant's-eye view: the underview, as it might be seen by an ant.

binding: sewing, stapling, or taping the finished pages to make a book.

biography: information about the author/illustrator. This may be placed on page 1 or on the inside or outside of the back cover.

bird's-eye view: the overview, as it might be seen by a bird.

book mock-up: a page-by-page rough copy of the book, based on the storyboard. Characters have no detail. Words are not used.

camera angles: different points of view, such as horizontal, bird's-eye, ant's-eye, close-up. A variety of camera angles adds interest.

close-up: an enlargement of a small part of a character or scene, such as a hand, eye, key-hole, or door-knob.

collage: a design or composition of various materials (colored paper, cloth, cutouts of magazine pictures) glued on a plain or patterned surface.

copyright notice: a small 'c' enclosed in a circle, followed by the name of the author/illustrator and the year in which the project was completed.

cover: includes the title in large letters and the names of the author and illustrator (if someone else did the artwork).

double-page spread: a single picture or design spreading across facing pages.

editing: correcting or changing items in the storyboard, book mock-up, or written story.

endpapers: the inside of the front and back covers and sometimes their facing pages. These areas may be used for decorative purposes or left plain. The author's biography may be placed on the inside of the back cover.

frame: one of the 28 small squares in the storyboard.

horizontal view: the horizon line and the characters and objects along it.

page turn: the suspenseful moment of turning the page, especially in a 'pattern' book.

paste-up: pasting or glueing the typed or word-processor copy onto the appropriate pages of the final book.

plot: see *storyline.*

pop-ups (see-throughs, peep-holes, pull-downs, fold-outs): techniques involving parts of the page that may be moved physically.

publisher's information page: page 2, opposite the title page. This page includes the copyright notice and dedication.

stick figures or circle characters: sketches that have little or no detail.

storyboard: a grid of 28 small squares, or frames. The first represents the front cover; the last, the back cover. The next two represent endpapers. Then come the publisher's information page (frame #2) and the title page (frame #3). Frames #4 - #24 are for story planning. Words are *not* included, but short lines may be drawn to indicate where words will go later.

storyline or plot: what happens in the story.

title page: page 3, the reverse side of the first page of the story. This page includes the title, without illustration, the names of the author and illustrator (if someone else did the artwork).

turnaround: the climax or turning point in the story. This usually occurs in the area of frames #11 to #15.

wraparound: one-piece protective cover that wraps around a book. It includes both front and back covers.

Recommended Picture Books

Picture books range from today's soft, nontoxic, washable cloth varieties to the more durable board books with plastic-coated, or laminated, pages. Some picture books have no words at all and some have movable parts — pop-ups, peep-throughs, pull-downs, foldouts. Some focus on letters or numbers or rhymes; others, on concepts, themes, and stories.

We encourage children to look at and read, where text is present, a wide variety of picture books. Although not all of these will serve as models for our storyboarding approach, many have brilliant artwork and intriguing text.

In some picture books, more accurately called illustrated books, the pictures are usually placed on separate pages facing the text and serve primarily to illuminate the text. Ian Wallace's *Chin Chiang and the Dragon's Dance* (Groundwood, 1985), Robin Muller's *The Sorcerer's Apprentice* (Kids Can Press, 1985), and Ron Berg's *The Owl and the Pussycat* (North Winds Press, 1984) are outstanding examples of the illustrated book.

The picture book model for our storyboarding project, however, is one in which text and illustrations are of equal importance and are totally integrated. An acclaimed critic of children's literature, Selma Lanes, makes this point metaphorically in *Down the Rabbit Hole* (Atheneum, 1971). The picture book "bears resemblance to Siamese twins: the words cannot stand independent of the illustrations nor, in theory at least, can the pictures without text. Separately, their contribution is thin, incomplete. Together, they comprise a fully satisfying experience." (Quoted in *Choosing Children's Books*, by David Booth, Larry Swartz, and Meguido Zola, published by Pembroke, 1987).

The picture books in the following selected list exemplify the artistry in both story and design that we promote in our workshops with students and teachers.

In these books you will find strong storylines, suspenseful page turns, varied viewpoints (horizontal, bird's-eye, ant's-eye, close-up), textured pages, purposeful design (including double-page spreads), and imaginative plots. Flegling authors and illustrators will find these positive features worth emulating in their own picture books.

Andrews, Jan. *Very Last First Time*. Illustrated by Ian Wallace. Groundwood, 1985.

An Inuit child goes mussel hunting on the seabed under the ice when the tide is out.

Illustrations full of mystery; unusually dramatic use of colors — purple, red, green, ochre; marvelous viewpoints; impressionistic watercolors add information that is not in the text; many double-page spreads.

Baker, Jeannie. *Where the Forest Meets the Sea*. Greenwillow Books, 1987. Australia: Julia MacRae Books, 1987.

Evocative; incredibly textured with sand, bark, sticks, modeling paste, paper, etc.; the highly detailed illustration of a rain forest makes the reader/viewer do a double-take — it looks like a photograph at first glance.

Baylor, Byrd. *When Clay Sings*. Illustrated by Tom Bahti. Macmillan, 1972.

Dynamic, inventive, graphic page design and type; three colors — brown, beige, black with gray — used exquisitely; native American feeling.

Bianchi, John. *The Bungalo Boys: Last of the Tree Ranchers*. Bungalo Books, 1986. Distributed by Firefly Books.

A wonderfully crazy story; variety of viewpoints; cartoon style; loose watercolor and black ink line artwork in keeping with the zany story;

mixture of double- and single-page spreads.
   See also *The Bungalo Boys: The Princess Frownsalot* (1988).

Brown, Marcia. *Shadow*. Collier-Macmillan, 1982. Retold from an African tale.

Bright, bold, dramatic, spooky, mysterious; full-color collage illustrations.

Brown, Margaret Wise. *The Runaway Bunny*. Illustrated by Clement Hurd. Harper and Row, 1972. The first edition appeared in 1942.

Gentle, whimsical, magical; two pages of text with black-and-white illustrations alternate with full-color double-page spreads.

Browne, Anthony. *Piggybook*. Alfred A. Knopf Inc., 1986.

Whacky story with surprise ending; simple text; delightful contrast of illustrations on each page turn; many different viewpoints; impressive close-ups.

Cleaver, Elizabeth (illustrator). *The Mountain Goats of Temlaham*. An Indian legend retold by William Toye. Oxford University Press, 1969.

Bold, colorful, dynamic illustrations done with textured, patterned, and hand-colored papers — torn and cut; many double-page spreads.
   See also *How Summer Came to Canada* (1969).

Downie, Mary Alice. *How the Devil Got His Cat*. Illustrated by Jillian Hulme Gilliland. Quarry Press, 1988.

Dynamic, beautiful, black-and-white silhouette illustrations; variety of viewpoints; book design and illustrations are so spectacular that color is never missed.

Dr. Seuss. *The 500 Hats of Bartholomew Cubbins*. Scholastic, 1938.

A classic; an offbeat masterpiece; black-and-white illustrations; color red used for the hat only — must be an important hat!?; variety of viewpoints; cartoon style.

Dr. Seuss. *Scrambled Eggs Super!* Random House, 1953.

A non-stop series of viewpoints and crazy characters; black-line brush drawings; the colors red, blue, and yellow create dynamic and unusual effects; visual repetition of two eggs — two birds.

Gay, Marie-Louise. *Rainy Day Magic.* Stoddart, 1987.

Wild, crazy illustrations; full of action; varied viewpoints; strong contrasts of shape, tone, and color.

Gergely, Tibor. *The Great Big Fire Engine Book.* Western Publishing Company, Inc., 1950.

Action drawing on large pages; the sparse text concentrates on sound.

Gilman, Phoebe. *The Balloon Tree.* Scholastic-TAB, 1984.

Ingenious use of decorative borders and page layout; detailed, humorous, full-color illustrations; takes inspiration from the Renaissance.

Hanson, Joan. *I'm Going to Run Away.* Platt & Munk Publishers, 1977.

Single lines of witty text adorn colorfully illustrated pages; effective selection of single- and double-page spreads.

Hearn, Emily. *Franny and the Music Girl.* Illustrated by Mark Thurman. Second Story Press, 1989.

Bright, clean, full-color collage illustrations throughout; use of graduated colored paper, textured and patterned paper with details shaded in colored pencil; variety of viewpoints; centrefold double-page spread.

See also *Race You, Franny* and *Goodmorning Franny, Goodnight Franny* (The Women's Educational Press, 1986 and 1984, respectively).

Jonas, Ann. *The Quilt*. Greenwillow Books, 1984.

Beautiful, full-color illustrations; haunting images; many double-page spreads and dramatic points of view.

Jonas, Ann. *The Trek*. Greenwillow Books, 1985.

Magical double-page spread illustrations; animals hidden in the art-work; bold shapes and textures; dynamic watercolors.
    See also *Round Trip* and *Now We Can Go* (Greenwillow Books, 1983 and 1987, respectively).

Keats, Ezra Jack. *The Snowy Day*. Penguin/Puffin Books, 1962.

Full-color, multi-media collage illustrations; masterful use of bold color, texture, and white space; rhythmic, elegant page design.
    See also *John Henry, an American Legend* (Penguin/Puffin, 1965; Scholastic, 1970) and *Whistle for Willie* (Viking, 1964 and Puffin/Penguin, 1980).

Kennedy, Richard. *Song of the Horse*. Illustrated by Marcia Sewall. Dutton, 1981.

Dynamic black-and-white compositions done on scratch board; exceptional examples of foreground, midground, background; illustrations full of excitement, action, and movement.

Kovalski, Maryann. *Brenda and Edward*. Kids Can Press, 1984.

Soft toned, loose, full-color illustrations; a black ink outline accents important details and borders the illustrations; variety of viewpoints; several double-page spreads.

McKlosky, Robert. *Blueberries for Sal*. Viking Press, 1948. Reprinted by Puffin Books, 1976.

Single color, dark blue-black illustrations; variety of dynamic view-points; illustrations have the expansive and dynamic quality of the outdoors.

Munsch, Robert. *The Paper Bag Princess*. Illustrated by Michael Martchenko. Annick Press, 1982.

Great story with a traditional beginning but a surprise ending; whacky, simple, full-color watercolor illustrations; traditional text/illustration page format.
    See also *A Promise Is a Promise* (Annick, 1988).

Newlin Chase, Edith. *The New Baby Calf*. Illustrated by Barbara Reid. Scholastic-TAB, 1984.

Highly textured plasticine illustrations; bright colors; beautiful design; humorous points of view; traditional text/illustration page format.

Oakley, Graham. *The Church Mice Adrift*. Macmillan, 1976.

Humorous, highly detailed, full-color illustrations; blend of realistic and cartoon-style drawings; multi-imaged page layouts; strong sense of sequence and animation.

Roughsey, Dick. *The Giant Devil Dingo*. An Australian aboriginal legend. Macmillan, 1973.

Simple, primitive, powerful images of the Australian outback; complementary colors sienna red and green (plus a varied pallet of pastel reds, pinks, and greens) are used effectively throughout the book; people, birds, and tree trunks, painted in a dark brown/black, stand out dramatically from the red-green background and at times look like calligraphic photographs; all double-page spreads.

Sendak, Maurice. *Where the Wild Things Are*. Harper and Row, 1963.

A classic in all respects; gentle yet dynamic, wild and crazy full-color illustrations; minimal text; the story starts with a small frame, centre page, which grows until it covers three double-page spreads where the wild rumpus occurs; illustrations get smaller as the plot goes back to reality; at wake-up time supper is still hot (no picture).

Shulevitz, Uri. *Dawn*. Farrar, Straus and Giroux, 1974.

Elegant watercolor illustrations; a small blue oval grows slowly page by page until dawn arrives in a double-page spread in full-color glory; minimal but poetic text.

Staunton, Ted. *Taking Care of Crumley*. Illustrated by Tina Holdcroft. Kids Can Press, 1984.

Full-color, cartoon-style illustrations; interesting borders where part of the action breaks out of the border; variety of viewpoints; traditional text/illustration page format.
    See also *Puddleman* (illustrated by Maryann Kovalski), 1983. A revised text with illustrations by Brenda Clark was published by Kids Can Press in1 988. The two editions make interesting comparison.

Stinson, Kathy. *Red Is Best*. Illustrated by Robin Baird Lewis. Annick Press, 1982.

Simple, clean, black outline drawings; color red predominates, as expected, and the eye follows it throughout the book; focus is on a single child at floor level.

Tejima, Keizaburo. *Fox's Dream*. Philomel Books, 1987. Originally published in Japan.

Beautiful, bold, dynamic woodcut illustrations; clean, simple colors and composition; strong sense of texture and line; full of action; minimal text.

Thurman, Mark. *Old Friends New Friends: Two Pals on an Adventure*. NCP (New Canada Publications), 1985.

Double-page spread illustrations with smaller illustrations incorporated to continue and modify the action; variety of viewpoints; multi-image double-page spreads suggest elapsed time.

Thurman, Mark. *Some Sumo*. NCP (New Canada Publications), 1988.

Detailed watercolor illustrations with patterned Japanese paper; variety of dynamic viewpoints; multi-image double-page spreads; unusual page design and text arrangements.

Van Allsburg, Chris. *Jumanji*. Houghton Mifflin, 1981.

Dramatic yet subtle tone drawings; numerous shades through black, gray, and white conte (chalk-based) pencil; wonderful viewpoints; traditional text/illustration page format.

Van Allsburg, Chris. *The Polar Express*. Houghton Mifflin, 1985.

Exquisite, full-color, textured, chalk pastel drawings; marvelous viewpoints; traditional text/illustrations page format; all double-page spreads bordered with a black ink outline.
See also *The Garden of Abdul Gasazi, Ben's Dream*, and *The Mysteries of Harris Burdick*.

Wagner, Jenny. *John Brown, Rose, and the Midnight Cat*. Illustrated by Ron Brooks. Kestrel Books/Penguin Books, 1977.

Gentle, sensitive pen-and-ink drawings rendered over soft pastel watercolor washes; different points of view showing both interior and exterior of a house; strong use of texture and pattern; double-page spreads.

Wallace, Ian. *The Sparrow's Song*. Penguin Books Canada, 1986.

Impressionistic, pointillistic watercolors; dramatic and unusual use of purple and green; variety of viewpoints; traditional text/illustration page format.

Waterton, Betty. *Mustard*. Illustrated by Barbara Reid. Scholastic TAB, 1983.

Humorous black-line drawings with the color brown added; variety of viewpoints; many double-page spreads.

Wildsmith, Brian. *The Circus*. Oxford University Press, 1970.

Bold, dynamic, highly textured, full-colored, multi-media collage illustrations.

See also *Wild Animals* (Oxford University Press, 1967).

Wynne-Jones, Tim. *Zoom Away*. Illustrated by Ken Nutt. Groundwood, 1985.

Dynamic, detailed crosshatched pencil drawings; unusual scenes; variety of viewpoints; traditional text/illustration page format.

See also *Zoom at Sea* (Groundwood, 1983).

Storyboard

The storyboard project described in this book is based on a 24-page book (a total of 28 frames, including front and back covers — inside and outside). For young children or for other projects, the format may be modified to 12 pages (16 frames, including covers — inside and outside), 10 pages (14 frames, including covers), or even 6 pages (8 frames — three double-page spreads and outside covers only). Four storyboard formats are provided here for your convenience.

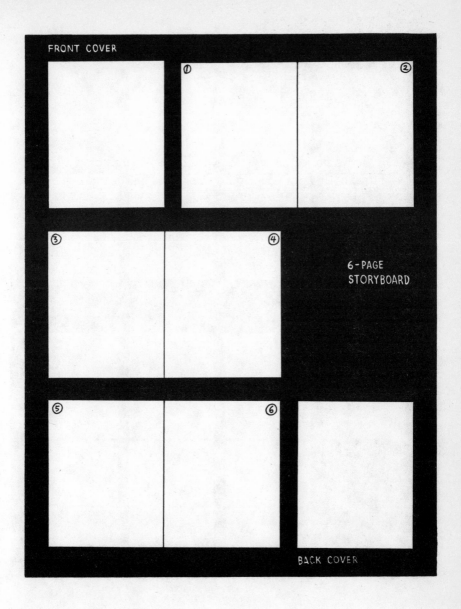

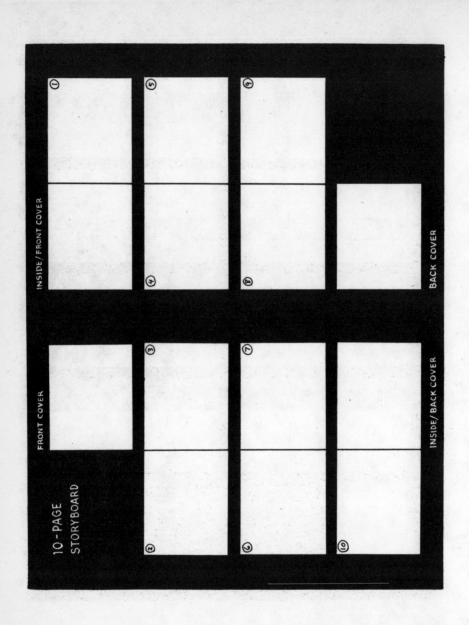

10-PAGE STORYBOARD